Eamonn McCabe:
SPORTS PHOTOGRAPHER

Eamonn McCabe:
SPORTS PHOTOGRAPHER

Geoffrey Nicholson

FOREWORD BY
Hugh McIlvanney

AURUM PRESS

TO RUTH
for her encouragement and tolerance

Photographs © Eamonn McCabe 1982
Text © Geoffrey Nicholson 1982

Published by Aurum Press Limited
11 Garrick Street, London WC2E 9AR

ISBN 0 906053 39 0

Designed by Neil H. Clitheroe
Prints by David Watkinson

Phototypeset by Tradespools Limited, Frome, Somerset
Printed by Balding & Mansell, Wisbech, Cambridgeshire

Previous page: Li-Chen Shi, Edmonton, London, 1978

FOREWORD
Hugh McIlvanney

Working with Eamonn McCabe can be hazardous to a reporter's ego. McCabe's photographs often convey the essence of an event or a performer with such dramatic succinctness that the writer assigned to the same job is left with the feeling of having turned in a 1500-word caption. My ability to cope with this sense of redundancy has been developed over twenty years of operating with a series of brilliant photographers whose work has appeared in the *Observer* alongside my words.

That training taught me to brace myself for humbling comparisons every time I lifted the paper. Fortunately, the first glance at the printed results of our labours frequently comes on a Saturday night in The Cockpit, the pub in which hacks and smudgers (Fleet Street's favourite term for photographers), wearied by the ceaseless pursuit of truth and beauty at the *Observer* next door, gather for refreshment. Bracing yourself is easier there.

During my first days as a news reporter I had to fight against a natural feeling of resentment that photographers invariably make it to the pub before writers. It took me a year or two to acknowledge unreservedly that there is a special strain on the photographer that entitles him to the release he enjoys once his film is delivered. The strain is identified with the awareness that he has only a few seconds, perhaps only a fraction of a second, in which to get his day's work right. If a reporter fails to see or hear something crucial connected with his story, some retrospective checking, maybe just a telephone call, can usually make good the deficiency. But the photographer who has missed the key shot is quite likely to find the lapse irretrievable. It is one of McCabe's major strengths that he allows himself very few lapses. With a regularity that is unnerving he comes back from the job with the best picture imaginable. And by that I mean the best picture *he* could have imagined, which is usually something far more interesting than would have occurred to the rest of us.

Sometimes he sets himself apart by making his the only lens to capture historic moments, such as the sinking of a Boat Race crew, or by a vividly original glimpse of a familiar ritual, like the picture of a table tennis player preparing to serve while the tiny white ball hovers, remote as a planet, above his head. Often he demonstrates his talents with portraits that can be read like biographies. But at least as outstanding are those photographs in which several performers are caught in intense, inter-related attitudes, perhaps half a dozen footballers or rugby players fixed in the moment when they are reacting with fierce individuality to some decisive incident. These shots have the quality of the best possible freeze-frame from some marvellously exciting movie: they are vibrant with a sense of hectic action crowding in from both sides of the moment they depict. They are, in short, compellingly alive, and to manage that effect consistently on a Sunday paper sports page is an extraordinary achievement.

It goes without saying that anyone who is up to his armpits in awards at 33 is liable to be a touch obsessive about his craft. But there is a great deal more to Eamonn McCabe than an insatiable eye for the striking image. An interesting nature houses the remarkable talent. I certainly feel that any story I set out to cover, whether it is on the other side of the world or on the other side of Blackfriars Bridge, has more chance of coming out right in the paper if I have Eamonn as an ally in the field.

Wales *v.* Australia,
Cardiff, 1981

In 1972, at the age of 23, Eamonn McCabe was employed taking pictures of pop stars. Or to be more exact, he was employed to print the pictures of pop stars taken by Alec Byrne, his boss at the London Photo Agency. But when concerts clashed, as they frequently did, McCabe was sent to the one Alec Byrne didn't want to attend, and gradually he came to spend more time with a camera than a pair of plastic tongs in his hands.

He had been a regular photographer for only two years, during which he had served an informal apprenticeship with the photo unit of a London college. It had been useful and agreeable but not very stimulating. In contrast the break into the pop world had been exciting, especially for someone of McCabe's age. 'The Rolling Stones, The Who, the Beach Boys – they were our heroes. Theirs was the music we listened to, anyway. It was worth travelling all over the country, and then travelling back through the night, to hear them; and there was a rawness about them that made good pictures. At the time I didn't want anything better than I was doing.'

Yet within a year there came a change, not so much in McCabe's attitude as in the pop world itself. The Gary Glitters and the Alvin Stardusts arrived: the hype bands with their carefully built images and routines. 'After a few months I found I wasn't getting anything out of photographing them. There was no incentive at all to drive up the A1 to one of their concerts at Leeds. It would be exactly the same act as I had seen at the Albert Hall, and I'd come back with exactly the same pictures. Nothing unexpected ever happened.'

In the building where McCabe worked was another agency, now called Sporting Pictures. He got to know the people there, and just when he was finding it more and more difficult to keep up his enthusiasm for pop photography, they asked him to cover the occasional football match for them.

They had picked the right man. McCabe had always been mad on sport, a follower of Spurs since he was at school, and still a devoted Sunday morning footballer. Eventually he might have found his way into sports photography without prompting. But it was the immediate contrast with his usual pop subjects that got

Brendan Foster, Crystal Palace, London, 1978

**Vitas Gerulaitis,
Wimbledon, 1981**

home to him – after the stale repetition of the concert stage, the unpredictable variety of the football field. 'I didn't know what I would get at any game; even if it was the same team as last time, or even the same fixture, it would make totally different pictures.'

Shortly afterwards McCabe moved on from the agency, and although it was not immediately into full-time sports photography, that was now the direction in which he was heading. By 1974 he had formed his own photo agency in north London, dealing mainly with sport. Two years later his work was appearing regularly in the *Guardian*. Another year and he was on a retainer with the *Observer*. Within a decade, while he was still only 33, he had three times won the title Sports Photographer of the Year.

It is not surprising that McCabe had no early ambition to become a sports photographer. When he was at school there was no such animal: most sports pictures were taken by newsmen drafted in to watch and wait by the goal-mouth on a Saturday afternoon. Even now it is a limited profession. There are excellent photographers specialising in particular sports – Patrick Eager in cricket, Colin Elsey in rugby, for instance – and several versatile people who can turn their hand to sport. But there are only five recognised posts in sports photography in the national press – three in the popular papers and two in the heavies. And there are only four British photographers who have – despite the apparent contra-diction – specialised in general sport and, by the fresh perception of their work, made a name far beyond it.

The first three are Gerry Cranham, whose photographs made their first impact in the *Observer* but who has since turned more to colour; Chris Smith, another ex-*Observer* man, now with the *Sunday Times*; and the late Ed Lacey whose pictures were seen, though too often uncredited, on almost every sports page in the country. Eamonn McCabe is the latest, and not the least, of them.

A Londoner of Irish background and rather Nordic appearance with blond hair and beard, McCabe is one of those fortunate people who seem totally at ease in their working world. He finds that a quality Sunday paper provides the ideal conditions for his work: time to prepare and exhaust all the possibilities on mid-week feature stories, combined with the quickening pressure of a deadline on Saturdays. He acknowledges, too, that the *Observer* in particular has not only allowed but encouraged him to develop a strong personal style.

He has met the expression 'an Eamonn McCabe picture' often enough to accept that such a thing exists in many people's minds, though he finds it hard to define to his own satisfaction. Humour and line are obvious components. So is a strong journalistic sense. McCabe doesn't often miss *the* picture; sometimes, as in the 1978 Boat Race, he is the only one who takes it. But there is something else too.

Perhaps it is that McCabe has gone back to a very basic type of photography. During the 1970s there was a great deal of experimenting, with sports photographers trying wider angles, fish-eye lenses and unconventional viewpoints, some of which McCabe has used himself. But in his more characteristic photographs he tends to close in tight to record the expression on the face of the player or athlete, the surprise, elation, despondency, fatigue. As a result his pictures are powerful in form and feeling. They emerge from the print around them with a candid appeal to the emotions.

McCabe looks on himself as a newspaper photographer, not an artist. It doesn't bother him unduly that sometimes he has to sacrifice technical perfection for the sake of immediacy. In fact what particularly pleases him is that he has won his three awards with 'working pictures'. All were taken on normal *Observer* assignments, in whatever light and under whatever constraints there happened to be. None was specially taken to strengthen his portfolio. Sports photography is his job, and it is by his working pictures, grain and all, that he would choose to be judged.

The alacrity with which Eamonn McCabe made up his mind to specialise in sport was in sharp contrast to the long and seemingly random process of trial and error which had led him to photography in the first place.

Born in Hampstead in 1948, he was brought up in Finsbury Park (as was the war photographer, Don McCullin, although that's just a

Hurling, Cork, 1980

Ricky Villa scores against Manchester City, Wembley, 1981

England *v.* Scotland amateur boxing, London, 1980

Water polo, Olympics, Moscow, 1980

coincidence, not a connection) where his parents ran a boarding house and later a hotel. The long hours they worked, and their dependence on the customer's beck and call, put him off the idea of joining them in the family business. Instead, at 16, he went into a solicitor's office.

It was an arbitrary choice. His schooldays, in Crouch End and at Challonor's in Finchley, had largely been spent in cheerful, busy idleness, playing football, picking teams, boxing. It was only in his fifth-form year that he began to take an interest in the law, and by then it was too late to muster more than a couple of O-levels.

Still, they were enough to start him on the way towards decent respectability as, perhaps, a solicitor's managing clerk. The trouble was that he found he didn't want it; the work was too studious and uneventful. After only six months he decided to switch to the brewing trade where at least he would get out and about among the publicans. Or so he thought.

It was another false start. Under the Mann, Crossman training scheme he was meant to spend six months in each of the various departments and then graduate as an area manager in his early twenties. It was only when he had spent eighteen months in the ordering department that the penny dropped. He protested and was told that what the company really needed was order clerks. Feeling cheated, he resigned on the spot. 'I was lucky to get out when I did. I am sure there are people of my age, trapped by young families and mortgages, who have stayed there as order clerks ever since.'

His next job, as boy Friday in an advertising agency, was a bit more like it. David Bowie had been a junior there before him, which was promising. There was a lighter atmosphere and more variety than he had known at work before. And for a couple of years it suited him well enough. 'What turned it sour for me in the end was seeing people getting fired any time we lost an account. It didn't affect me directly. As the dogsbody I had the safest job in the firm, and anyway I wasn't looking for security. But I couldn't stand the harshness of it. Added to that, I'd got the travel bug.'

It was California that attracted him: 'Everything seemed to be happening there, and I wanted to go and have a look.' So at 19,

Margaret and Frank Price, 1979

**Kenny Dalglish,
Liverpool _v._
Aberdeen, 1980**

Tony Doyle, Herne
Hill, London, 1979

Nellie Kim,
Olympics, Moscow,
1980

with a few hundred pounds that he had saved and borrowed and the promise of help with local introductions from a Santa Monica antique dealer he had met in London, he set out to hitch-hike across the United States. The next months, when he worked simply to pay his way and not with any thought of a career, were to make all the difference to the way his life shaped.

McCabe didn't take to Los Angeles or its Santa Monica suburb, but he fell in with someone who was travelling north to San Francisco. There he shared a house with some college students, and it was they who suggested that he should come along and see what it was like at an American university. What followed could have happened only in the United States, perhaps only in California.

Having read the syllabus McCabe was attracted by three of the subjects offered: modern English (which was largely devoted to the lyrics of The Beatles and Bob Dylan), psychology, and film-making and the history of film. He knocked at the doors of the professors who ran these courses and asked if he could sit in on their classes. Not one of them turned him away, although he wasn't offering to pay fees and had no formal qualifications for entering university. He was told that he wouldn't be able to earn any credits, but as he was so keen he could come in and learn.

So for the next five months, from eight in the morning until noon, he attended lectures like any other student, accepted for his cheek and his novelty, and serving as the resident Englishman off whom the rest of the class bounced their ideas. And, since his savings had run out, he worked by night as a bus boy and washer-up in a restaurant.

The class in which he became most involved and received most encouragement was film-making. 'The professor had once worked in a Soho strip club; perhaps that's why he felt some sort of sympathy for me.' As part of the course he was expected to produce a four-minute film each week, for which he bought a second-hand Super-Eight movie camera, as well as his first battered Nikon to take his 'holiday pictures'. The film had to have a self-contained story line, and since no sound was edited on to it, it had to be set to recorded music.

McCabe remembers making his first few films sitting on the kerb, shooting everything below knee height. As far as he knew it had never been done before, and since even the shoes and the clothes, the car and bus wheels, were different from those back home, he could see them with a fresh eye. Later the plots of the films became more elaborate, with the students at his digs joining in as actors and collaborators. 'Somebody would say, let's do a murder. And somebody else would say, okay, let's have a murder in a public lavatory, and so on, all of us feeding off each other's ideas. My role, though, was always as cameraman.'

After four or five months the professor, who was also attached to UCLA, *the* film school in California, advised McCabe to move back to Los Angeles. There he would be able to attend a better course, and probably combine it with a job in the film industry. He was tempted, and but for one inconvenient factor, that might well have been the start of a career in the film industry. But the year was 1969 and the Vietnam war was on.

By staying on officially in the United States McCabe would have become a Class A1 alien, and almost certain of an early call-up to fight for a cause for which he, like most of his contemporaries in the student world, had little sympathy. An alternative was simply to go to ground. 'America is an easy place to lose yourself in, but only as long as you want to stay there. The moment you try to leave the country, they find you out.' Some members of Adam Faith's backing group were currently in San Quentin jail because their papers weren't in order.

The other option was to return straight away to London, and with some backward glances that is what McCabe decided to do.

Once home he was frustrated to find that there was no outlet for his new enthusiasm for film-making. He couldn't get into the industry, and he was no longer living within that easy, accommodating student circle which had backed him up in making his own films. There was only one thing to do: concentrate on stills photography where he could be self-sufficient.

Well aware that he was raw at the game, he looked for a job

**Rugby League try,
Wembley, 1978**

Kevin Keegan
scores against
Scotland, Wembley,
1979

Jim Watt *v.* Alexis
Anguello,
Wembley, 1981

Chris Kamara,
Saracens, 1980

Butch Wilkins,
Chelsea, 1976

**Hang gliding,
Dorset, 1978**

which would teach him the essentials, the chemistry and the f-stops. He found it in a 'Wanted' ad for an assistant in the photo unit of the Physics Department at Imperial College, London. At 21 he was comparatively old to be taken on as a beginner; at the same time he had little in the way of experience to offer. But again it was his eagerness that appealed to Keith Hobbs, head of the unit, and under his guidance McCabe was able to spend the next couple of years learning a wide range of basic skills – processing and printing, taking portraits of the students, photographing bits of space craft, copying slides for lectures.

Apart from providing the ideal grounding it was also a comfortable job, with security, regular hours, five weeks' holiday, annual rises, and use of the college swimming pool and squash courts. But if anything it was too comfortable, and after a while McCabe, nagged by the feeling that to remain might be taking the easy way out, jumped off to land on the wobbling stepping-stone of pop photography. 'Mind, later I often felt that I'd been daft to let the Imperial job go; but there was some drive in me to get out from under it.'

Even when he left the pop world about a year later, McCabe wasn't yet ready to commit himself full-time to sport. He had his Saturday afternoon rugby lined up, but to make weekends meet, and also to widen his experience, he took another assistant's job. This time it was with the American, Robert Golden, who combined photo-journalism (he was building up a record of working-class life in Britain) with still-life photography, mainly for book jackets.

The journalistic side of Golden's work appealed strongly to McCabe: 'I think that is where I got hooked into newspaper work, though in my case the leaning was towards sport.' But studio work held his interest only briefly. 'I discovered I wasn't that technical a photographer. The painstaking business – setting up tripods and constantly reshooting to get the effect just right – wasn't in my character. I remember the jacket we did for the Schumacher book, *Small Is Beautiful*; it was an egg with a globe in it. We had to photograph the two separately, then put them together to get the shadow work so perfect that you couldn't tell that the globe wasn't actually inside the egg. I'm not saying that it wasn't enjoyable at

**Qamar Zaman,
Wembley, 1981**

England *v.* Wales,
Twickenham, 1982

**Maradona and
Stielike, River Plate
Stadium, Buenos
Aires, Argentina,
1982**

first to work to these fine standards, but after five or six months I had to admit that it wasn't really me.'

By then, as it happened, Golden had to take a period off work with a knee injury, and it suited them both that McCabe should move on. And now at least McCabe knew in which direction he wanted to move – towards sport and journalism. Early in 1974, operating from his home in Wood Green, he set up the North London Photo Service.

'That's how, in a muddled few months, it all came together, though I don't suppose I was properly aware of it at the time. I pooled what I had learnt about agency work with the knowledge I had gained from Bob about photo-journalism. But until the last moment everything had still been wide open. I'd met Ruth, my wife, soon after I got back from America. She was teaching, and there was even the thought that she would write biology and zoology books and I would illustrate them. I might have gone down almost any avenue if I had found some satisfaction.

'It's funny, I get a lot of letters from people asking me how to become a sports photographer. Should they get a job on a local paper? Should they take a photography course? And I usually say that if they've got the chance of getting into Ware College, for instance, they should take it. That certainly wasn't my way, but how can I tell them that the thing to do is first go into a solicitor's office, then a brewery, and afterwards hitch-hike around America for a few months . . .?'

Even before he set up his own agency, McCabe was paying occasional visits to the nearby Saracens rugby club and selling the pictures to the local press. That was to be the basis of his new business: Saracens rugby, Southgate hockey, Spurs and Arsenal football, to be offered to the *Hornsey Journal*, the *Hampstead and Highgate Express*, the *Islington Gazette* and one or two other papers on the fringe of his area. From one event he might get four pictures published. And since sport was concentrated into the weekends, in between he would cover fires, prize-givings and 'Runaway Car Hits Market Fruit Stall'. It might be irksome hanging around all evening to get a picture, worth no more than £5, of a

Lester Piggott, Ascot, 1977

darts tournament winner holding his trophy. But the more McCabe worked, the more he earned, and as the agency he had built from nothing flourished, so it began to represent financial security.

It became hard to give up, but so did his unfaltering ambition to become a regular sports photographer on a major paper. His first approach was to send stock pictures and portraits to Fleet Street; perhaps months later one or other of them would be used, and the first he would know about it was when a cheque came through the post. Then he found that if the Saracens were playing a fashionable club like London Welsh, the pictures were sometimes of interest to rugby papers like the *Daily Telegraph* or the *Guardian* – at least it was worth taking prints round to their offices early on Sunday afternoons.

But when, for the third year running, McCabe found himself photographing the Lord Mayor giving out badges to the Boys' Brigade, he knew he had reached the end of his local tether. Without closing the north London agency, simply farming out surplus work to other photographers, he moved his dark room from his home to King's Cross, conveniently closer to Fleet Street. And under the new name of Photosport, he set out to cultivate the nationals. By 1976 the *Guardian* was using so many of his pictures that he felt justified in asking for future work to be commissioned, which it was at the rate of three or four jobs a week. As John Samuel, the *Guardian* sports editor, puts it: 'McCabe was a genuine photo-journalist, and when we were selecting an event or a personality to cover, his was just as important a voice as any of the writing staff.'

Even more might have come of the *Guardian* connection if, later in the year, McCabe hadn't noticed that Chris Smith's credits were no longer appearing in the *Observer* but were now in the *Sunday Times*. Wondering if there might be an opening, McCabe took his portfolio along to Gary Woodhouse, the *Observer* picture editor. As far as he could tell, Woodhouse was 'reasonably interested', but said that he was using someone else at the time. It was only at the end of an otherwise unpromising interview that Woodhouse asked him whether he was working that evening.

McCabe said that he had hoped to go to the England–Holland

Alan Minter, the Thomas A' Becket, London, 1979

**Severiano
Ballesteros wins
the Open, Lytham St
Anne's, 1979**

**Clint McGregor,
Richmond Athletic
Ground, 1979**

**Peter Bonetti,
Chelsea, 1978**

John McEnroe,
Wembley, 1981

Terry Griffiths and
Ray Reardon,
Stafford, 1980

game at Wembley, but had been unable to get a pass. The *Observer* did have a pass, and Woodhouse wondered whether he would like to cover the game for them, concentrating on the Dutchman, Johan Cruyff.

'I remember going off very excited, then after the match rushing back to King's Cross and processing the film until two in the morning to deliver it next morning. When I opened the *Observer* on Sunday, there was a strip of my pictures right across the page. I was elated. Five pictures from my first job; I thought I must be in there. Then came the let-down. It was three months before I heard from them again.'

What he heard was that the other man had left, and the sports photographer's job was once again vacant. McCabe was never formally invited to take it, but after a few months he had built up from one commission a week for the paper to two or three. 'At that point I decided to let the King's Cross darkroom go and rely on things working out at the *Observer*. It may seem strange to people in other occupations, but that's the sort of decision you have to take. Sunday papers have always been a freelance world where you don't so much get offered jobs as gradually ease yourself into them and make them your own. Once you have got your foot in the door you need to be available for anything. It was what I most wanted to do, and was worth the risk.'

Much of the *Observer*'s strong appeal for McCabe was that he would be succeeding Chris Smith on a paper where Ed Lacey had also been frequently employed. These two photographers had influenced him more than any others. 'Chris I admired because he had never been one of the pack, always separating himself and working on his own. There were his innovations, in particular the silhouette. And although, except on rare occasions, I kept away from that because it was almost his trade-mark, I felt that he had given me a licence to shoot sport in an individual way. What I also find admirable about him is that he's still as keen as a 17-year-old amateur. If there are two of us running round the touchline to get a picture, the other one is always Chris.'

Beryl Mitchell, London, 1981

**Ilie Nastase,
Olympia, London,
1980**

46

If Smith was already an established staff man when McCabe got to know his work, Ed Lacey was still the remorselessly energetic freelance whose work appeared everywhere. His influence was in pioneering close-up action photography with the extremely cumbersome equipment then in use. 'Long lenses weren't very fast but they were heavy. Nowadays they are only 18 inches long, and although we've got monopods for support we still moan about them. Ed's lenses were three or four feet long. The man must have been extremely strong just to hold them.'

Studying the *Observer* every week, McCabe was absorbing the influence of the paper's other photographers, especially Neil Libbert and Jane Bown. One of the pictures in this book, Ladies' Day at Ascot (p 74), might well have been taken by Jane Bown, as McCabe acknowledges. 'I am sure I was looking towards that scene, knowing that there must be a subject there, because I had seen similar pictures by Jane. What amused me about it first was that it obviously hadn't been that particular lady's day. And then this Beau Brummel character came walking in from the right to provide the final element.'

Altogether McCabe was convinced that he would find a sympathetic atmosphere at the paper, and he was not disappointed. 'The *Observer* uses its own photographers and picks them for their style. And because of that it relies on their judgment. In the popular press if Paul Mariner scores three goals then you must have a Mariner picture. And I'm not saying that I might not come back with one myself. But if for me the picture of the game was a completely isolated incident involving two backs, nobody would reproach me. Nobody would ask, where's Mariner? There I'm fortunate. I get the impression that on, say, the *News of the World*, if a dog comes on and pees against the Arsenal goalposts, that's the picture they must have. And if their own photographer hasn't got it, they'll buy it in from an agency.'

Willie Carson,
Leicester Races,
1980

For the sports photographer, as for the sports writer, Sunday paper journalism is like working for two separate publications: a weekend feature magazine which is put together with care but no

**Alex Higgins,
Wembley, 1981**

Severiano
Ballesteros,
Wentworth, 1981

consuming urgency from Tuesday to Friday; and on Saturday a set of sports news pages produced to even tighter deadlines than apply to the daily press. McCabe says he enjoys this regular change of tempo.

'At midweek events, say international football matches, I have time to cover the whole of the play and then wait, if need be, until the managers are leaving. Daily paper people would give their arm to do that, but they have to be in their cars and on the way to the office ten minutes before the finish. At a tennis tournament I can cover a match which starts at seven in the evening, which is too late for them.'

On Saturdays the tables turn. In fact to catch the first edition with a football or rugby picture, McCabe must take it within ten minutes of the start. There's a messenger waiting by the corner flag to whip the film back to the darkroom. 'Even if the play is down the other end I have to get something; there's a hole in the paper to fill. I can then spend the next hour getting a more considered picture for the main editions. But even that must be printed up by six o'clock; on a daily the deadline would be nine. Still, it's not a hardship. Frankly I like to have one day a week working under pressure. Five days must be a strain. But I don't think I'd care to work on a magazine where there was never a need for the instant result, as I have on a Saturday with the *Observer*.'

The weekly routine varies, but Tuesday is generally given up to planning stories and ordering passes. If the story is based on an interview, it is probably the writer who will make the contact and the appointment for them both. But if it centres around some scheduled event, McCabe will make his separate arrangements. He finds his work has two great advantages over that of the news photographer. 'While the newsman often goes out on stories that don't get used or don't make pictures, very few of our mid-week features get spiked. And while news can break anywhere at any time, a great many sports stories are diary items. You know exactly when the Cup Final or the Grand National will be, and you can be pretty certain when Coe will run against Ovett. You can plan ahead.'

Scotland qualifying for World Cup Finals, 1981

June Croft, Wigan,
1981

57

Henry Rono and
Nick Rose, Crystal
Palace, London,
1979

Big Daddy and
Giant Haystacks,
Wembley, 1981

Barnes and Ze Maria, England *v.* Brazil, Wembley, 1978

Jerry Walker, Wembley, 1977

59

What doesn't necessarily happen is that all possible facilities are laid on. If there's one thing McCabe envies American photographers it is the access that sporting bodies in the United States fall over themselves to provide. McCabe, for instance, used a remote-controlled camera in the goal to take his ice hockey photograph at the Streatham rink (p108). But he was allowed to do that only at a five-a-side training session; and although it would be perfectly safe and simple to take a similar picture at a Football League match, he knows that permission would be refused. Football's growing obsession with its image on the television screen due to advertising has made life increasingly difficult for press photographers, who have been moved back behind the advertising boards, and in some cases asked to work lying flat on their stomachs.

There is a constant battle for position. Wimbledon officials couldn't understand why McCabe, working for a Sunday paper, should need to take pictures on the centre court on a Friday. Even when he pointed out that Virginia Wade was on the point of winning the women's title, and that this would still be of some interest two days later, he was allowed to snatch no more than a couple of harassed pictures. At Twickenham photographers are free to work around the touchline only by rota; at one match in three they have to shoot from a seat in the end stand with just a head-on view of the play. Admittedly the problem is aggravated by the sheer number of those applying for a pass. But even when sports authorities try to help, they often make matters worse. At world events like the Olympics photographers often find themselves penned into a small area where each ends up taking virtually the same picture as his neighbour.

Since most sports pictures are shot out of doors, the weather can cause as much havoc as official indifference or awkwardness. Rain is a particular worry with modern cameras – 'with their electronic bits and pieces, they play up more than the old mechanical cameras when they get wet.' But bad weather was the making of a couple of McCabe's most gratifying pictures, taken when he covered his first Oxford and Cambridge Boat Race in 1978.

Rob James and Chay Blyth, River Thames, London, 1981

**Marvin Hagler,
Lavender Hill,
London, 1980**

63

On the accompanying press launch there are places available to photographers which most of the old hands ignore. They find the trip monotonous, and reckon that they can get better pictures, as well as a quicker exit to their offices, from the bank or the bridges. But McCabe decided that what he wanted was close-up pictures of the crews in action, so he went aboard, the only press photographer on the river.

'The start of the race was fine, then all of a sudden this cloud came over very low, and everything went black as though it was the end of the world. The rain poured down, the river got choppy, and you just knew that something was going to happen. If one of their boats didn't go down, I thought ours probably would. There were launches skippered by elderly gentlemen in pink school caps and scarves knocking into us and each other.

'It was Cambridge who got into trouble first, terrible trouble, and began to sink. I was using a long lens because I was a fair distance away, and I managed to get one shot in before it got covered in water. Then I went through the whole range of lenses – starting with a 400mm and ending up with a 24mm – because in that downpour there was no question of drying them out. In the end I could hardly see Cambridge, but I just let go with everything I had, clinging to the front of the boat and expecting any minute to be knocked into the river and dragged down by my cameras and rain gear. I'm not happy in the water at the best of times.'

McCabe did land safely and returned sopping wet to the *Observer*. 'Right, they said, six columns on the front page. But I wasn't even sure that I had salvaged anything. When I went to the darkroom there was just this one photograph taken on the long lens with the crew undoing their shoes as the boat went under. So that was the news page happy.

'But then sport were looking for something. And again I found the one usable neg on the wide angle: the Cambridge launch going to the rescue, and the crew standing up as though they were walking on the water. That was the lot. But we were the only paper with our own pictures; the others had to take them off television. And although I have seen technically better photographs, I will always think of that as a really good day's work.'

**Ian Botham,
England v.
Australia,
Manchester, 1981**

On the whole sports photography is not a dangerous profession – at least not compared with covering wars and revolutions. Most of the accidents that have befallen McCabe in the line of duty have been more comic than harmful: tripping headlong over one of his own straps in the middle of the Ajax stadium in Amsterdam, to the delight of the 40,000 Dutch spectators; being straffed with plastic bags of urine on the touchline at Cardiff Arms Park; and knocking out half a tooth when ducking into his camera to avoid a football at Highbury.

One sport offers more risks than most, however, and that is motor racing. 'If you put yourself on a bend where something's going to happen, then it could easily happen to you.' That was nearly the case when McCabe took his crash picture at Long Beach, California (p106). The circuit has a notorious first bend where the track doubles back on itself, and it is almost impossible for thirty cars to get round at speed.

'Because it was a well-known trouble spot a stand had been put up there so that photographers could cover the action; it only needed a medium telephoto lens. I was on it this particular day, and something did happen. Patrick Tambay's car came over the top of poor old Niki Lauda's, and the whole thing could easily have spilled over towards the stand. It was already swaying with the number of people on it, and if it had toppled on to the track we'd have made the headlines ourselves.'

There are only a few circumstances in which a photographer like McCabe hands over his film to be processed by someone else: when his first edition pictures are brought back by the messenger; when because of the distance (say from Troon or Aintree) his pictures are transmitted back by wire; or when he is abroad and has to air-freight his material home ahead of him. In every other case he is expected to develop his own film when he returns from a job. 'It's not that the darkroom people wouldn't do it if I asked; and when you've driven back down the motorway for a few hours, the last thing you want to do is process film. But I think it's right that it should be the photographer's own responsibility.'

Archer, London, 1980

**Croquet,
Hurlingham,
London, 1979**

69

Cambridge, Boat
Race, River
Thames, London,
1978

For one thing, a ruined negative cannot be repaired; so if anything goes wrong in the processing, the photographer has only himself to blame. For another, he knows more about the way he shot the pictures than he can possibly convey to anyone else. He might feel certain that there was a good picture on one roll, and that since he had shot it in bad light, it ought to be processed for a little longer. 'When you go into the darkroom yourself you can control the image. Not to mention that for me the great excitement of photography is still the moment when I hold up the wet negative to the light to see if I've got anything. If I lost that charge there wouldn't be any point in going on.'

McCabe also enjoys printing, and he does a certain amount at home. 'You need to keep in touch with photography through the darkroom, otherwise you lose your instinct for exposure. But it wouldn't be practicable for the photographers to print their work at the *Observer*. Besides, the guys in the darkroom there do it better. It's their profession.'

The prints, in the form of contact sheets, go up to the editorial floor where the picture editor (it is now Tony McGrath) makes the first selection. McCabe would normally be there to point out any frames which have a special relevance to the story.

Perhaps half a dozen pictures are then printed up, and the final choice of the one or more to appear in the paper rests with the picture editor and the sports editor; the latter also decides what space it will occupy. In theory – and in practice on some papers – the photographer has no further say in the matter, 'but obviously he is around there nudging.'

The choice could be, and often is, a cause of friction. Having conceived the picture and taken it, and then seen it through to the negative, doesn't McCabe find it frustrating to hand over control to someone else? 'Not really. Someone must have the final word, and editors are there to edit, I accept that. And don't forget that we have probably been talking about this picture for several days. We know what we wanted, and we know what we've got. The point is I am well treated, so are the pictures – and not just because I've won a few awards. From the earliest days I found that my best pictures were going in.'

**Jockeys,
Punchestown,
Republic of Ireland,
1980**

**Ladies' Day, Ascot,
1977**

74

Failed weightlifter,
Olympics, Moscow,
1980

What proportion of them would have been his choice? 'I would say about seventy per cent. I'm not claiming that there aren't some Saturday nights when I bite my tongue and go down to the pub to join the others feeling sore because the picture I liked hadn't made it. But the feeling doesn't last. On balance I'm happy, and that's why I'm still at the *Observer.*'

Eamonn McCabe's pictures refuse to fit into most of the traditional categories. He is a specialist, but not in the usual narrow sense: within his speciality there are a dozen or more sports which he turns to regularly, and many other minor ones which crop up now and again. At certain periods of the year, and within the space of a week, he might cover snooker, athletics, cricket and racing – activities which scarcely overlap except in time. For that variety he is grateful, even if he has to take a lot of it as it comes.

Action and Portraiture are other labels which can be misleading in McCabe's case. Few of his action pictures fail to portray character, and equally few of his portraits lack activity, even if it is only the features which are mobile.

Nor is it generally helpful to divide his work into mid-week features and Saturday's visual reporting; the compartments are anything but watertight. The picture of Maradona soaring over Stielike's tackle (p 34) was taken to complement a football feature by Hugh McIlvanney from South America. But if McCabe came back with a photograph like that from a Saturday match, nobody would think of it as 'soft' or 'featurish'. It would simply be complying with his basic aim: 'To stop the reader and turn him into a viewer for a little while – get him to *look* at what is happening.'

What helps to blur the distinctions is that McCabe very rarely carries a picture in his mind when he approaches his subject. 'I like to go to an event or a training session and get whatever I can from it. In some sports, like hang gliding or motor racing, I may have a definite picture in mind. I knew, for instance, that I was going to take that particular sort of picture of the cycling at the Moscow Games (p 10); I was aware of the lines of that part of the circuit and used a fish-eye lens to emphasise them. But generally at football or rugby I prefer to react to what I find.

'I don't think I'm especially quick at capturing pictures, but I am quick to see a picture. I can usually tell that the people beside me are shooting differently. They are going for the header of the ball while I might be trying for an expression of joy or anger. And I believe that I often see a shape in things, an arrangement of limbs and bodies, which others don't find interesting.'

A good example of how the elements compose themselves in his mind is his picture from the Wales v. Australia match (p 6). 'I could see that Terry Holmes, the Welsh scrum-half, was being pulled back and was dropping the ball, and that's what I was into. But at the same time I was aware of the other players in the background looking on, and it seemed a definite picture. But I couldn't have told you about their expressions, or whether the third player from the right, or whatever, had a beard. It was just an impression.

'It was only when I got to the negative (again, the joy of seeing the negative for the first time) that I knew it had worked. It's such a narrow line. A tenth of a second either way and it would have been totally different.' Someone once called it McCabe's Last Supper, perhaps facetiously, but it does have the strange formal quality of a bas relief.

In action pictures you don't get a second chance and you have to take conditions as they are, including the light and the setting. 'You are always governed by backgrounds – whether there is an exit sign or an advert which will take the eye from the picture. At Arsenal, for instance, there is a constant problem. You have to work from one side of the pitch or else you're shooting into the sun. But then the light picks out the stand opposite which has some very noticeable balconies. The only thing is to shoot down the pitch, not across it, and try to use the patch of black background where the other stand throws a shadow over the field. Or maybe I'll try to work in the shady area altogether rather than in the bright light. It's not too bad in mid-winter, but there's a special problem at the beginning or end of the season.'

Sometimes McCabe is able to turn bad light to his own advantage. His picture of the Chinese table-tennis player Li-Chen Shi (p 3) was taken at a hall in Edmonton, north London, where the artificial light was appalling, and since he never uses flash he

**Liverpool win the
European Cup,
Paris, 1981**

Les Cocker and Don Revie, Wembley, 1977

Golders Green Sox baseball team, London, 1977

Bob Willis, Lord's
Cricket Ground,
London, 1978

Table tennis yoga,
1980

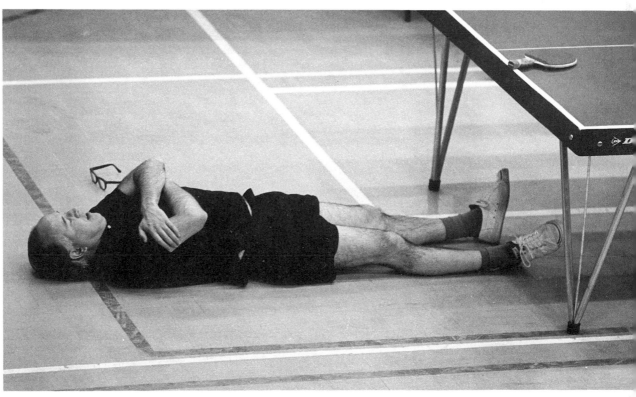

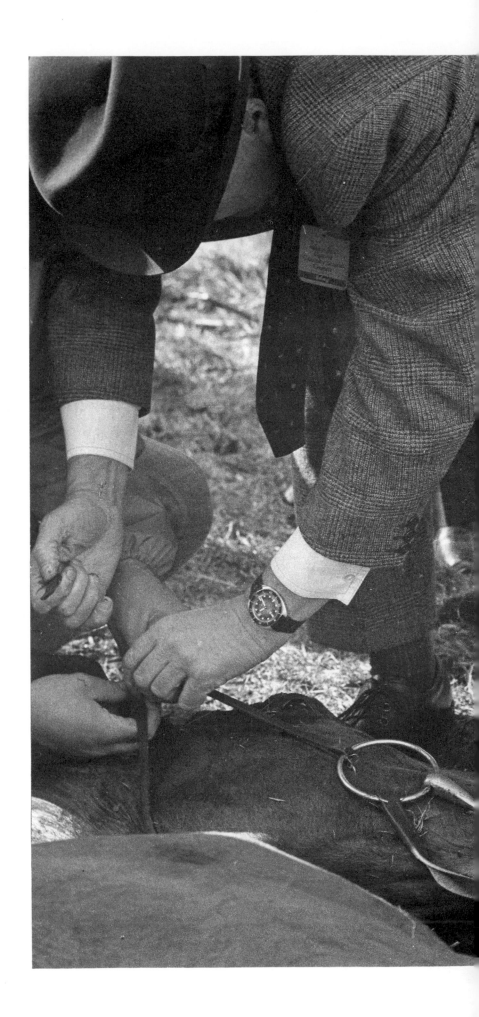

Jonjo O'Neil and
Alverton, Grand
National, Aintree,
1979

84

wondered whether he would get a picture at all. But then he noticed that occasionally Li-Chen threw the ball high into the air when he served. At that moment not only did the ball catch the dim overhead light, but so did the player's upturned face. McCabe moved round – again to get rid of an obtrusive exit sign – hoping Li-Chen would repeat the high serve. When he did, it was the ball apparently suspended in mid-air, the impassive concentration of the player's features, and the obliteration of every unnecessary detail which made this photograph so effective.

McCabe sees many of his pictures just looking around without a camera to his eye, as in another from table tennis (p 83), this time taken in the undramatic qualifying rounds of a big tournament. 'I noticed that every now and again this guy would lie down on the floor between games, and it amused me. He was a middle-aged man being beaten by a 14-year-old. At ground level it made a messy picture with all the other players' legs and the table legs, so I went on the balcony to clean up the background and shoot straight down on the floor. Luckily for me he not only repeated his yoga but arranged his bat on the table and his glasses on the floor perfectly. It just summed up the atmosphere of the day.'

This is not to say that McCabe simply waits for things to happen. He believes, when he can, in walking the course, attending any rehearsals. It wasn't exactly premeditated, but it wasn't fortuitous either when McCabe got a picture of Princess Anne falling at the water jump in the Badminton horse trials last summer. He hadn't been to a three-day event before, so he took the trouble to seek advice from the local experts and then stationed himself at a point by the lakeside where a good deal of activity was promised. Even without the Princess's splash-down, McCabe had a number of good pictures from the day.

Without having done his homework, too, he would never have been able to take his photograph of Torville and Dean ice-dancing at Stockholm (p 98). 'This is one of the hardest events to capture, partly because of the speed of movement and the size of the rink, and partly because when you see one of the skaters clearly the other often has his face turned away. So I went to watch

Knockout, Rainbow Theatre, London, 1978

British Open Polo Championship, Cowdray Park, 1982

Mike Brearley, The Oval, London, 1978

90

them practising their routine the day before, and I knew there was just one moment when her face fell back into the lens, and the effect was extremely romantic and stylish. Next day I knew when this moment would come, and where, and I was able to position myself for it.'

In portraiture McCabe has a little more control over circumstances, but the picture of Alan Minter (p 39) is one of the very few he has posed. 'What I wanted that time was a strong picture of a fighter still covered in sweat from training, so I just stood him there and asked him to look straight into the lens.' Normally he prefers to catch his subject going about his normal business. The photograph of Mike Brearley (p 90) illustrates his more accustomed approach.

'There is some mystique about the England cricket captain which is much more than just a matter of scoring centuries, and what I was trying for was a picture which said this. Dressing rooms are usually taboo to photographers, especially at Lord's; but when Middlesex were playing Surrey at The Oval, which is more informal, Brearley agreed to let me come in for just five minutes.

'At first he was on the balcony writing letters in his ordinary clothes. Quite a good situation, and appropriate enough to Brearley the philosopher. But I had hoped for something more. Then suddenly the Middlesex batting collapsed and Brearley was on. I asked if I could take some pictures of him padding up, and he said, all right, just a couple. I knew he meant exactly that; he knows just what he wants. So I stayed there in the corner until he went for his kit to a big trunk covered in stickers. It was a time when Brearley must have been living out of suitcases for months. And beyond that the trunk seemed to conjure up a kind of boarding school atmosphere. It was not a picture which would have done for anyone; you would have needed to show someone like Botham in action at the wicket. But for Brearley it was perfect. It summed up the nature and the way of life of the man.'

Given his preference for working on his own and observing from a distance, it is perhaps not surprising that McCabe has a soft spot

Basketball, Crystal Palace, 1981

**Coe and Ovett,
Olympics, Moscow,
1980**

**Canoeing, Reading,
1982**

**John Watson,
Silverstone, 1981**

Tigers ladies'
basketball team,
Hemel Hempstead,
1979

Cross-country,
Crystal Palace,
London, 1981

for minor sports. 'The big events don't excite me as much as people might expect. Photographing the Olympics or the World Cup is all very well, I wouldn't want to miss them; but with one or two hundred other photographers there it's a bit like working on a production line. To me photographing the cricket tourists arriving at Arundel is just as satisfying. Or doing a croquet tournament at Hurlingham with just a few spectators watching. There are fewer restrictions, and the pictures you get are not so hackneyed. In any case I work for a very English newspaper and these are very English sporting events.

'I feel rather the same about working abroad. Obviously it's good to see, and to photograph, the top people performing at the very highest level. If you are interested in sport you are bound to respond to that. But there is also a slightly artificial pressure to it. Just because the paper has spent so much money to get you there you feel you have to take great pictures, but there's no guarantee that you will send back anything better than if you'd gone to Stoke-on-Trent. I don't have to go to a big event to get keyed up, and if someone said there'd be no more foreign trips for me, I'm not sure that I'd be desperately unhappy.'

There are some photographers who can't resist the latest piece of gadgetry; given half a chance they'll be off to buy another lens, a new all-purpose camera case. McCabe doesn't share their obsession with equipment. 'I don't really think that's what makes or breaks a picture. It's the eye that sees it and takes it. Almost the worst mistake you can make in photography is to pay too much attention to what other people are using, to think that because they have a certain film or a particular lens that's the only way to do it. In fact the general quality of equipment is now so high that the choice is even less important. I'm supposed to be at the top of the tree, if you like. But when I go along to a football match there will be twenty youngsters just as well equipped as I am.'

McCabe has one old Leica M2 to which he is much attached; its quiet, unobtrusive shutter is ideal for times when he wants people to forget he is there. Otherwise he has used conventional 35 mm cameras ever since he bought his first camera in California, and

Torville and Dean, World Championships, Copenhagen, 1982

**Steeplechase,
Olympics, Moscow,
1980**

Karen Robb,
Watford, 1978

always with manual focusing. He can see the value of an auto-focus camera like the Canon 90 for certain 'news' jobs – if, for instance, he was trying to snatch a picture of a football manager rushing past him into the stadium. But he wouldn't trust auto-focus for long-distance sports work. 'You could never be certain whether it was picking out a footballer on the pitch, or had decided that it was the grandstand behind which made the picture.'

Similarly McCabe has no time for automatic exposure. He has cameras with an automatic mode, but he has never used it. Constantly shooting in black and white, he reckons to be able to read the light unaided and so expose the film just as he wishes. Sometimes he consults the camera light meter for confirmation, but if it has the cheek to contradict him, he overrules it and trusts his own judgment. Except, that is, when he is shooting colour.

'It's very difficult to get black and white far wrong – I mean, get a complete loss of image – and what I go for is a fairly heavy negative in an attempt to get more on it. But you can't afford to do that with colour; the range is narrower and if you over-expose you end up with wishy-washy colours instead of what you hope for, a richness of tones. In effect, using colour you have to go the other way. And so, because I find it difficult to shoot against my nature, I rely on the meter to correct it.'

He uses motor-drive extensively, though not only for taking sequence pictures. Of more value is that it allows him to keep the camera to his eye, and so not lose the chance of another picture by taking it down to wind on. Fish-eye lenses he employs sparingly, zoom lenses not at all. He has no interest in their trick effects, and for straightforward use they have two defects: their lens speed is slower than he needs, and their double action is clumsy. 'By the time you have made both adjustments, the game has moved on.'

Although he knows that many press photographers have changed over to Ilford HP5, McCabe sticks with Kodak Tri-X film. It's true he won the Ilford £1000 award a few years ago, but that was on film he borrowed when he ran out. 'I don't see any reason to change for change's sake, or just to try and win the award again. I find Tri-X a good, tough working film.'

His range of equipment he suits to the assignment, but he has a basic survival kit. It consists of two motor-driven cameras and one ordinary body as a back-up. Then he always takes a long, a medium, a portrait and a wide-angle lens of some description; if he senses the need he might augment them with an extra wide-angle and an extra telephoto. Tennis he tends to shoot on 400mm for baseline shots and 180mm for the net; and if he has a favourite lens to which he constantly turns it is his 400mm f3.5 – his 'Ed Lacey lens', as he calls it.

What McCabe regards as the governing factor in sports photography is shutter speed. 'I try to use the fastest I can, not only to freeze the movement but, in games like football and rugby, to get the ball as close as possible to the subject. If the light, for instance, was a 500th at f5.6 at 400 ASA, I would use a 1000th at f4. I would prefer to give up a stop in depth of field and go for the faster speed.' This loss of depth can also be complementary to another of the constant needs of sports photography: to blur the background. 'As long as you can separate the subject from the background, there is an extra advantage in throwing the crowds and hoardings and grandstand seats out of focus. In newspaper reproduction the cleaner the image the better. The worst pictures you see are the ones with too much going on.'

To carry his equipment McCabe uses either a heavy silver case, which can double as a seat, or else a canvas shoulder bag – 'though I'm beginning to get a bit worried about the weight I'm carrying on my shoulders; there have been several reports recently about the heart and back troubles it can cause. From that point of view a backpack would be ideal, but you couldn't get at your lenses quickly enough.' Inside there are few surprises. A chamois leather for drying off rain-soaked cameras. A monopod to bear the weight of long lenses and also, in the long trudge around golf courses, to serve as a carrying handle on his shoulder: 'After a day at golf your neck muscles get very tight.' Maybe, too, remote-control devices for taking photographs from positions where he is not allowed or wouldn't care to stand – under an Aintree jump, for instance. And some paper on which McCabe has been known to write captions. 'To be honest I can't claim to be very good at that.

Patrick Tambay,
Long Beach Grand
Prix, California,
1979

Women rowers,
Kingston upon
Thames, London,
1980

High jumper,
Olympics,
Moscow, 1980

ce Hockey goal,
treatham, London,
981

Ed Moses, World
Cup, Rome, 1981

Cycling, Olympics, Moscow, 1980

**Exhausted rowers,
Henley, 1979**

113

My excuse is that while I'm jotting down notes I might be missing a good picture. But I do make a point of it at cricket, where the fans are always anxious to know whether that was the stroke that got Botham his fifty.'

Sport can't be adequately covered in the Cartier-Bresson manner: a couple of taped-up Leicas stuffed into an overcoat pocket. The pace of the action and the distance from the touchline to the centre of the field pose problems which can only be solved by motor-drive and long lenses. But McCabe is far from being a gadget freak, and in comparison with many he travels light.

Nobody who has known McCabe before and since he won his series of awards will have noticed much outward change in him. Perhaps he is a little more confident, but then he never lacked professional assurance. And certainly he has too much natural good humour to become vain. McCabe knows that it suits him to be part of a team, and he remains a considerate, congenial man to work alongside.

On the other hand he grants that there are dangers in winning too much recognition too soon. 'I am grateful for what the prizes have done for me. They have helped to get me established in the business, and a bit more widely known, and I think they have helped the paper. What they also do is put you under a certain competitive pressure, which can be good for you.' Two things stopped that pressure from becoming a burden. One was *not* winning the Sports Photographer of the Year award for a third successive year in 1980. The other was winning it again in 1981.

'I admit I'd love to get it for a fourth time, but it's not that important to me any longer. I don't think it will make me a bad photographer if I don't – any more than it makes the others bad photographers if they don't. I've carved my small niche, and now it's my own pride in my work which will have to carry me through. What I must do is set my own standards and keep working.'

Certain photographs have so far eluded him. There is the classic boxing picture: 'The thump on the jaw and the spray of sweat coming off the feller's head; just for my own satisfaction I'd like to get one of those.' One reason he hasn't managed it yet is

**Daley Thompson,
Crystal Palace,
London, 1979**

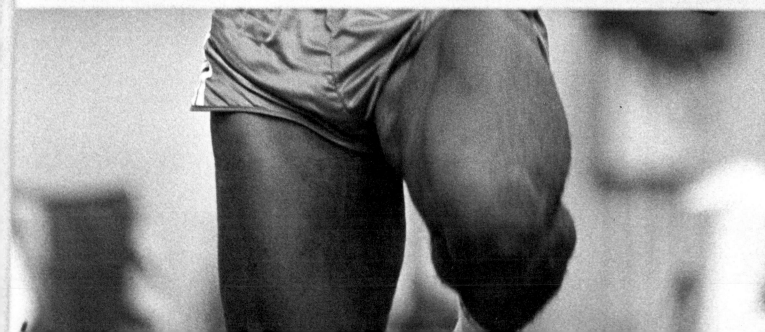

Phil Meeson,
Aerobatics World
Championships,
1982

that big fights rarely take place on a Saturday, and when McCabe comes to live boxing it's practically a new experience. 'It's such a quick sport, and I feel my timing is a little bit late. You have to anticipate the punch, and it's only regular boxing photographers who know when somebody's shoulder is coming back.'

In a totally different context McCabe feels that the start of the *Observer*'s own transatlantic yacht race has somehow got away from him. After several attempts from the air had failed to produce a strong picture he decided in 1982 to photograph it at sea-level, but a minute before the start of the race his motor launch broke down and he was left stranded on the starting line. Real tennis, with its tiny figures on the long indoor court, he has also found fiendishly difficult. 'If you concentrate on the player you just make him look like another McEnroe or Borg; what you can't capture at the same time is the curious atmosphere of the game.'

These are some of the specific challenges left to McCabe. But beyond them lies the general development of his approach to sports photography. 'Now that I have got wherever I have with the direct close-up, maybe I can afford to experiment and go a little wider.' But it is far more likely that McCabe's style will unconsciously and gradually evolve than that it will take a sudden lunge in a new direction.

The great temptation for specialist photographers is to become engrossed in technique and innovation at the expense of the subject. But that is unlikely to be McCabe's way. He remains essentially a sports fan, excited by the game and the people who play it. After ten years his enthusiasm for recording some vital quality about them is unblunted. 'I still think that the most important picture I have ever taken isn't last week's, or any in this book. It's the picture I'm going to take next Saturday.'

APPENDIX

(The numbers refer to the pages on which the photographs appear)

3 Li-Chen Shi, Edmonton, London, 1978
85 mm, f2 lens, Ilford HP5 film rated 1600 ASA, 60 th at f2
This picture was taken in a hall that had very little lighting. I noticed that this player would throw the ball up every now and again while serving, and his face would then be caught by the light available. The bonus of this picture was the ball captured so high and the clean background.

6 Wales v. Australia, Cardiff, 1981
400 mm, f3.5 lens, Kodak Tri-X film rated 800 ASA, 1000 th at f4
This picture has been likened to the Last Supper: it is not a great rugby photograph but it captures the faces and feelings that are the essence of the game.

8 Brendan Foster, Crystal Palace, London, 1978
400 mm, f3.5 lens, Kodak Tri-X film rated 1600 ASA, 250 th at f3.5

10 Vitas Gerulaitis, Wimbledon, 1981
180 mm, f2.8 lens, Kodak Tri-X film rated 400 ASA, 1000 th at f8

14 Hurling, Cork, 1980
400 mm, f3.5 lens, Kodak Tri-X film rated 800 ASA, 1000 th at f5.6

Ricky Villa scores against Manchester City, Wembley, 1981
300 mm, f2.8 lens, Kodak Tri-X film rated 1600 ASA, 500 th at f2.8

15 England v. Scotland amateur boxing, London, 1980
85 mm, f2 lens, Kodak Tri-X film rated 1600 ASA, 500 th at f2.8

Water polo, Olympics, Moscow, 1980
400 mm, f3.5 lens, Kodak Tri-X film rated 400 ASA, 1000 th at f8

16 Margaret and Frank Price, 1979
180mm, f2.8 lens, Kodak Tri-X film rated 800 ASA, 500th at f4
In this picture I wanted to show how reliant Margaret is on her husband Frank – here he is holding the wheel chair down so that she does not fall out with the effort of throwing the discus.

18 Kenny Dalglish, Liverpool v. Aberdeen, 1980
135mm, f2 lens, Kodak Tri-X film rated 1600 ASA, 500th at f2.8

20 Tony Doyle, Herne Hill, London, 1979
105mm, f2.5 lens, Kodak Tri-X film rated 400 ASA, 250th at f16 (panned)

21 Nellie Kim, Olympics, Moscow, 1980
180mm, f2.8 lens, Kodak Tri-X film rated 1600 ASA, 500th at f2.8

24 Rugby League try, Wembley, 1978
180mm, f2.8 lens, Kodak Tri-X film rated 800 ASA, 500th at f4

26 Kevin Keegan scores against Scotland, Wembley, 1979
85mm, f2 lens, Kodak Tri-X film rated 800 ASA, 500th at f4
After a goal is scored in a big game the joy of the player scoring can say just as much as a picture of the actual goal. Here Keegan ran straight towards me (lucky for me – he could have run the other way), and the contrast between Keegan and the Scottish players says it all.

Jim Watt v. Alexis Anguello, Wembley, 1981
85mm, f2 lens, Kodak Tri-X film rated 1600 ASA, 500th at f2.8

27 Chris Kamara, Saracens, 1980
400mm, f3.5 lens, Kodak Tri-X film rated 400 ASA, 1000th at f5.6

Butch Wilkins, Chelsea, 1976
400mm, f5.6 lens, Kodak Tri-X film rated 800 ASA, 500th at f5.6

28 Hang gliding, Dorset, 1978
180 mm, f2.8 lens, Kodak Tri-X film rated 400 ASA, 500th at f5.6

34 Maradona and Stielike, River Plate Stadium, Buenos Aires, Argentina, 1982
300 mm, f2.8 lens, Kodak Tri-X film rated 1600 ASA, 500th at f2.8

40 Severiano Ballesteros wins the Open, Lytham St Anne's, 1979
400 mm, f3.5 lens, Kodak Tri-X film rated 800 ASA, 500th at f5.6

31 Qamar Zaman, Wembley, 1981
180 mm, f2.8 lens, Kodak Tri-X film rated 1600 ASA, 250th at f2.8
I used a medium telephoto lens to try to capture a collision between the two squash players – a risk shooting so tight because one could end up cutting off heads or arms.

36 Lester Piggott, Ascot, 1977
105 mm, f2.5 lens, Kodak Tri-X film rated 800 ASA, 500th at f4

42 Clint McGregor, Richmond Athletic Ground, 1979
400 mm, f3.5 lens, Kodak Tri-X film rated 400 ASA, 1000th at f5.6

Peter Bonetti, Chelsea, 1978
400 mm, f3.5 lens, Kodak Tri-X film rated 800 ASA, 1000th at f5.6

32 England v. Wales, Twickenham, 1982
300 mm, f2.8 lens, Kodak Tri-X film rated 800 ASA, 500th at f2.8

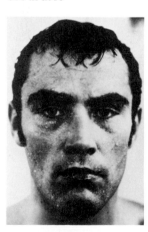

39 Alan Minter, the Thomas A'Becket, London, 1979
85 mm, f2 lens, Kodak Tri-X film rated 800 ASA, 250th at 2.8

43 John McEnroe, Wembley, 1981
300 mm, f2.8 lens, Kodak Tri-X film rated 1600 ASA, 500 th at f2.8

46 Ilie Nastase, Olympia, London, 1980
180 mm, f2.8 lens, Kodak Tri-X film rated 1600 ASA, 250 th at f2.8

54 Scotland qualifying for World Cup finals, 1981
85 mm, f2 lens, Kodak Tri-X film rated 1600 ASA, 250 th at f2.8

Terry Griffiths and Ray Reardon, Stafford, 1980
35 mm, f2 lens, Kodak Tri-X film rated 1600 ASA, 60 th at f2
I was trying in this shot to capture the atmosphere of snooker. I would have preferred there to be a cue in the picture somewhere but I still feel it conveys the feeling of the sport.

49 Willie Carson, Leicester Races, 1980
400 mm, f3.5 lens, Kodak Tri-X film rated 400 ASA, 1000 th at f5.6

56 June Croft, Wigan, 1981
300 mm, f2.8 lens, Kodak Tri-X film rated 800 ASA, 250 th at f4

50 Alex Higgins, Wembley, 1981
300 mm, f2.8 lens, Kodak Tri-X film rated 1600 ASA, 250 th at f2.8

44 Beryl Mitchell, London, 1981
300 mm, f2.8 lens, Kodak Tri-X film rated 400 ASA, 1000 th at f5.6

52 Severiano Ballesteros, Wentworth, 1981
400 mm, f3.5 lens, Kodak Tri-X film rated 800 ASA, 500 th at f4

58 Henry Rono and Nick Rose, Crystal Palace, London, 1979
400 mm, f3.5 lens, Kodak Tri-X film rated 400 ASA, 1000 th at f8

Big Daddy and Giant Haystacks, Wembley, 1981
35 mm, f2 lens, Kodak Tri-X film rated 1600 ASA, 250th at f2.8

59 **Barnes and Ze Maria, England v. Brazil, Wembley, 1978**
180 mm, f2.8 lens, Kodak Tri-X film rated 1600 ASA, 500th at f2.8

Jerry Walker, Wembley, 1977
24 mm, f2.8 lens, Kodak Tri-X film rated 1600 ASA, 250th at f2.8
The face of defeat said more about the game of basketball I had just watched than all the pictures I took of the winners celebrating.

60 **Rob James and Chay Blyth, River Thames, London, 1981**
300 mm, f2.8 lens, Kodak Tri-X film rated 400 ASA, 1000th at f5.6

62 **Marvin Hagler, Lavender Hill, London, 1980**
85 mm, f2 lens, Kodak Tri-X film rated 800 ASA, 250th at f2.8

65 **Ian Botham, England v. Australia, Manchester, 1981**
600 mm, f5.6 lens, Kodak Tri-X film rated 800 ASA, 500th at f5.6

66 **Archer, London, 1980**
180 mm, f2.8 lens, Kodak Tri-X film rated 800 ASA, 500th at f2.8

68 **Croquet, Hurlingham, London, 1979**
400 mm, f3.5 lens, Kodak Tri-X film rated 400 ASA, 1000th at f8
I watched this player Mullinger Minor for a while and noticed that he would leap down and line up the balls with the hoop whenever he was close to one. I stalked him for half an hour and next time he did it I was waiting for him.

70 **Cambridge, Boat Race, River Thames, London, 1978**
400 mm, f3.5 lens, Kodak Tri-X film rated 1600 ASA, 250th at f3.5

73 Jockeys, Punchestown, Republic of Ireland, 1980
24 mm, f2 lens, Kodak Tri-X film rated 1600 ASA, 250th at f2.8

74 Ladies' Day, Ascot, 1977
500 mm, f8 mirror lens, Kodak Tri-X film rated 800 ASA, 500th at f8

76 Failed weightlifter, Olympics, Moscow, 1980
400 mm, f3.5 lens, Kodak Tri-X film rated 800 ASA, 250th at f4
Another picture of a loser, but I feel it says more about weightlifting than a picture of a man lifting the bar above his head.

80 Liverpool win the European Cup, Paris, 1981
24 mm, f2 lens, Kodak Tri-X film rated 1600 ASA, 250th at f2

82 Les Cocker and Don Revie, Wembley, 1977
180 mm, f2.8 lens, Kodak Tri-X film rated 1600 ASA, 250th at f2.8

Golders Green Sox baseball team, London, 1977
400 mm, f3.5 lens, Kodak Tri-X film rated 400 ASA, 500th at f5.6

83 Bob Willis, Lord's Cricket Ground, London, 1978
400 mm, f3.5 lens, Kodak Tri-X film rated 400 ASA, 1000th at f5.6

Table tennis yoga, 1980
180 mm, f2.8 lens, Kodak Tri-X film rated 1600 ASA, 250th at f2.8

84 Jonjo O'Neil and Alverton, Grand National, Aintree, 1979
85 mm, f2 lens, Kodak Tri-X film rated 800 ASA, 250th at f2.8

86 Knockout, Rainbow Theatre, London, 1978
24 mm, f2 lens, Kodak Tri-X film rated 1600 ASA, 250th at f2.8

88 British Open Polo Championship, Cowdray Park, 1982
400 mm, f3.5 lens, Kodak Tri-X film rated 400 ASA, 1000th at f3.5

90 Mike Brearley, The Oval, London, 1978
35 mm, f1.4 lens, Kodak Tri-X film rated 800 ASA, 125 th at f2.8

92 Basketball, Crystal Palace, 1981
180 mm, f2.8 lens, Kodak Tri-X film rated 800 ASA, 500 th at f2.8

94 Coe and Ovett, Olympics, Moscow, 1980
400 mm, f3.5 lens, Kodak Tri-X film rated 400 ASA, 500 th at f5.6
I wanted to show where the race was won so I went to the last bend and captured Coe kicking for home. Unfortunately I missed the great picture at the finish, where Coe comes over the line with arms raised.

96 Canoeing, Reading, 1982
300 mm, f2.8 lens, Kodak Tri-X film rated 400 ASA, 500 th at f8

John Watson, Silverstone, 1981
16 mm, f2.8 lens, Kodak Tri-X film rated 400 ASA, 250 th at f5.6

97 Tigers ladies' basketball team, Hemel Hempstead, 1979
85 mm, f2 lens, Kodak Tri-X film rated 1600 ASA, 250 th at f2

Cross-country, Crystal Palace, London, 1981
24 mm, f2 lens, Kodak Tri-X film rated 400 ASA, 500 th at f8
I was trying to show in this shot the depth of the snow and how hard it was to trudge through it.

98 Torville and Dean, World Championships, Copenhagen, 1982
300 mm, f2.8 lens, Kodak Tri-X film rated 1600 ASA, 500 th at f2.8

100 Steeplechase, Olympics, Moscow, 1980
16 mm, f2.8 lens, Kodak Tri-X film rated 800 ASA, 500 th at f2.8

102 Karen Robb, Watford, 1978
50 mm, f1.4 lens, Kodak Tri-X film rated 1600 ASA, 250 th at f2.8

106 Patrick Tambay, Long Beach Grand Prix, California, 1979
180 mm, f2.8 lens, Kodak Tri-X film rated 400 ASA, 1000th at f8
Long Beach, a town circuit like Monaco, is notorious for tight bends – especially the first, when the cars are all close together. I positioned myself on this bend and caught the predictable crash.

108 Women rowers, Kingston upon Thames, London, 1978
180 mm, f2.8 lens, Kodak Tri-X film rated 400 ASA, 60th at f8 (panned)

Ice hockey goal, Streatham, London, 1981
24 mm, f2 lens, Kodak Tri-X film rated 1600 ASA, 500th at f2.8

109 High jumper, Olympics, Moscow, 1980
400 mm, f3.5 lens, Kodak Tri-X film rated 400 ASA, 1000th at f8

Ed Moses, World Cup, Rome, 1981
24 mm, f2 lens, Kodak Tri-X film rated 1600 ASA, 250th at f2

110 Cycling, Olympics, Moscow, 1980
16 mm, f2.8 lens, Kodak Tri-X film rated 400 ASA, 500th at f5.6
This road bend was a particularly good shape for a cycling picture and the fisheye lens I used exaggerated the shape, making it look as if the cyclists were going round and round a track circuit.

112 Exhausted rowers, Henley, 1979
180 mm, f2.8 lens and 1.4 converter, Kodak Tri-X film rated 400 ASA, 500th at f5.6

115 Daley Thompson, Crystal Palace, London, 1979
400 mm, f3.5 lens, Kodak Tri-X film rated 400 ASA, 1000th at f5.6
I wanted to capture the power and energy Daley Thompson puts in just before he jumps the hurdle, so I focused a foot before the bar to get this picture.

116 Phil Meeson, Aerobatics World Championships, 1982
16 mm, f2.8 lens, Kodak Tri-X film rated 800 ASA, 500th at f8
I took this picture hanging upside-down with a camera held over my head looking back at Phil Meeson